Journal Writing Activities

by Mark Springer

Illustrated by
Randy Rider

Publisher
Instructional Fair • TS Denison
Grand Rapids, Michigan

About the Book

Journal Writing Activities presents three broad themes that relate to middle school students' on-going quest to understand themselves and their place in the world. The themes involve a wide range of subject areas, and the writing activities are applicable to a variety of units and classes.

The purpose of the author is to provide topic ideas that allow the teacher to focus on any appropriate content and writing skills while simultaneously allowing students of varying abilities to be creative in their responses. Though grouped according to the complexity of the form, most suggested topics are open-ended to allow for many levels of difficulty.

About the Author

Mark Springer is a much published educator with over twenty years of teaching experience at the middle school level. He received his Bachelor of Arts in English from Haverford College. Mark also holds a Master of Arts in English from the University of Chicago.

Mark has been involved in the development of innovative curriculum in the areas of interdisciplinary humanities, English, art, creative writing, and American studies. For the past nine years, he has been co-teaching the well known WATERSHED Program, an interdisciplinary curriculum Mark was instrumental in developing, at Radnor Middle School in Pennsylvania.

Credits

Author: Mark Springer
Illustrator: Randy Rider
Cover Illustrator: Margo DePaulis
Project Director/Editor: Sharon Kirkwood
Editors: Dottie Clune, Barbara Kravitz
Production: Pat Geasler

Standard Book Number: 1-56822-284-X
Journal Writing Activities

2400 Turner Avenue NW
Grand Rapids, MI 49544

Table of Contents

Goals of a Journal Program

One excellent way of helping students learn to communicate effectively is through a directed journal writing program. Such a program sharpens students' language skills, widens their repertoire, builds their confidence, and helps them discover their relationships to the world around them. This makes the writing process a more personalized and enjoyable experience that encourages students to write more. Effective journal programs are carefully constructed to accomplish four interrelated goals.

Establish and maintain relevance—Writing exercises should always be grounded in the writers' experiences. Journal topics ought to be integral to the students' general learning experiences and relevant to the students' lives. Journal writing topics should flow logically and naturally from the students' other work. Nothing is worse than a journal that lacks coherence; nothing kills motivation and interest faster than writing assignments lacking personal significance. If the writer is not interested in his or her writing, no audience will be.

Reinforce content area knowledge—When journal assignments stem directly from students' general studies, they provide special opportunities for students to enhance that learning. Writing about the topics they are studying helps students internalize information, examine interrelationships, and synthesize conclusions. This leads to greater understanding and retention of the content covered. At the same time, using learning topics as the focus of writing assignments reinforces the writing process by providing pre-writing activities and background experiences on which the students can draw.

Motivate interest and encourage creativity—Effective journal assignments stimulate students to think in new and intriguing ways about the content under consideration. At the same time, these tasks allow students to use their creativity as well as their knowledge. This gives them a sense of control and a vested interest in the writing which, in turn, encourages students to write regularly.

Foster language skills development—By focusing on particular skills, by appropriately sequencing those skills, and by clearly establishing expectations, directed journal assignments move students toward improved writing skills and increased sophistication without frustrating them. The students know precisely what destination they should reach and can concentrate on effective strategies to get there.

The briefest look at these goals reveals the dynamic tension inherent in any journal writing program. The program must be structured for content and skill development, but it must remain flexible enough to meet the needs and interests of diverse learners. The same problem exists for a book of this sort. It must present concrete examples and ideas, but it cannot predict precisely what topics will best suit your students and your teaching situation.

So the real task is up to you, the teacher. You must view the ideas presented here as examples and adapt them to your students. The topics and writing forms presented can be adapted to an infinite number of subjects, as long as the four essential criteria discussed above are maintained.

Using This Book

Journal Activities is designed to help you develop and carry out a complete journal writing program for your students. The section of **Tips on Conducting a Journal Writing Program** provides general guidelines for developing your program. The **Forms and Worksheets** can all be adapted to your particular classroom situation; the twelve model forms and documents range from student goal sheets and journal-entry logs to information about proofreading symbols, as well as a sample letter to be sent to parents. The **Suggested Writing Activities** are organized under three theme areas. Ideas are presented for simple journal entries, short paragraphs, longer tasks, and supplemental activities.

Tips on Conducting a Journal Writing Program

- **Educate students and parents about the goals of the journal program.**

  a. Explain the program to students, distribute the forms, and explain each form.

  b. Send a letter to parents explaining the program and inviting their support.

- **Provide a regularly-scheduled time for writing.** The frequency and duration of writing sessions will vary depending on scheduling factors and skill levels. Some classes may be able to write daily, while others can schedule only a once-a-week session. Younger, less-experienced students may be able to sustain writing for only five or ten minutes, while older or more experienced writers can handle longer sessions. What is most important is that you set a time and maintain it, so that writing becomes a ritual.

- **Provide assignments which are appropriate to students' skill levels.** Identify appropriate themes and topics for your class, then establish a sequence of journal activities appropriate to your students' skill levels. (See the sample sequence and suggested writing activities on pages 10 and 11.) If you need to determine the basic skill levels of your students, give a preliminary writing assignment to assess the students' skill levels on the basis of their responses to the assignment.

- **For each writing assignment, focus on a limited number of specific skill areas.** As students become more familiar with the writing process, you can involve them in selecting the skill areas to be focused on. Practice in setting goals and expectations for their own work helps students become independent writers. Students' work will be more focused and productive if you limit the number of skill areas rather than asking them to consider many different skill concepts at one time.

- **Require students to keep all of their journal work in a special folder or binder.** Using a binder helps students develop organizational skills and monitor their progress. Materials in each binder should include the student's goal statement, required topics record sheet, and journal-entry log. (See *Forms and Worksheets* on page 9.)

- **Provide meaningful feedback on every paper you collect.** Your comments on your students' journal writings show whether you care about their work. Point out improvements as well as errors, and make concrete suggestions for changes.

- **Explain the evaluation criteria and process at the outset of the program.** How many journal entries will each student be required to submit to you? Will students have a voice in determining which entries are submitted? How will their work be evaluated? Will students be involved in peer reviews? Will there be opportunities for self-assessment? Will students be allowed to revise and improve their work?

- **Provide opportunities for students to share their work with a wider audience.** Writing requires an audience, and the wider the audience, the greater the incentive to write well. The possibility of publishing for audiences beyond the classroom—e.g., in a monthly newsletter, an anthology of the year's best, and/or magazines and newspapers—provides added motivation for students to write. Being published lends credibility and value to students' efforts.

- **Remember that your attitude establishes a tone that students quickly discern and emulate.** Be creative and enthusiastic and have fun!

Forms and Worksheets

- The **Letter to Parents** provides a model for a letter explaining your journal program to parents.
- **My Journal Writing Goals** is a form on which students record specific writing goals which can be evaluated (e.g., improving spelling, developing logical arguments).
- Use the **Required Topic Cover Sheet** to provide detailed instructions (e.g., purpose, special skill areas, date due) for assignments which you will collect from students. After you have completed the form, make copies of it and distribute a copy to each student.
- The **Record of Required Topics** helps students keep track of assignments which have been turned in.
- **Specific Skill Areas** describes four categories of skill areas: mechanics, style, organization, and content. Provide copies of this sheet for students to keep in their journals so they can refer to the information as they work on each assignment.
- **Proofreading and Correction Symbols** explains frequently used proofreading marks so that students will understand your corrections. Provide a copy for each student to keep in his/her journal for reference.
- **Troublesome Words** lists words which are frequently misspelled or misused. Provide a copy for each student's journal, and add to the list as the year progresses. Referring to the list helps students become aware of errors they can avoid.
- Students can use the **Journal Entry Log** at the end of each writing session to record a brief description of the day's journal activity. Provide a copy for each student's journal and distribute additional copies as needed as the year progresses.
- **Student Self-Assessment** sheets help students assess their own performance. Sheets are provided for assessing a specific required topic assignment, as well as for mid-year and end-of-the-year evaluations.
- The **Peer-Assessment Form** can be used when students evaluate each other's writing.

Suggested Writing Activities

The suggested writing activities in this book have been grouped into three theme areas: **My Body, My Place in History, and My World.** The theme areas relate to middle school students' ongoing quest to understand themselves and their place in the world. Each theme includes a variety of topics. Although the topics can be used individually, they also build upon each other to form a coherent approach to journal writing about the theme.

For each topic, suggestions are provided for three types of writing activities: simple entries, short paragraphs, and longer tasks. You can adapt these activities for a variety of units and classes, to focus on appropriate content areas and writing skills, and to accommodate students of varying abilities. Each theme section concludes with suggestions for supplemental activities, including both writing and non-writing assignments.

Feel free to make copies of the appropriate Suggested Writing Activities sheets as needed. In some assignments, students might be allowed to choose from the list of topics, and all students will appreciate the visual reference when working on any given assignment.

Sample Journal Writing Sequence

Simple entries would be identified as basic lists and label drawings.
Examples:

- List problems or diseases that can damage your skeleton.
- Draw and label a map of the original thirteen colonies.

Short paragraph assignments require more descriptive writing than simple entries.
Examples:

- Describe the differences between a red corpuscle and a white corpuscle.
- Select a twentieth-century amendment to the U.S. Constitution and explain how it affects you.

Longer tasks require more creativity, analysis and/or research.
Examples:

- Write a story describing a water droplet's experiences in the hydrologic cycle.
- Select two famous discoverers and write a conversation in which each tries to convince the other that his/her discovery was more important.

Supplemental activities may be used to enhance content area knowledge, broaden students' experiences within the subject area, and/or increase motivation. These activities make excellent group activities since many are major projects requiring many hours to complete.

- **Supplemental writing activities** are major assignments in which writing is the basis for an activity such as a play or is augmented by other activities such as creating illustrations. Many of the activities can be assigned as group tasks, for example:

  Planet Play—Write and perform a play in which the characters are continents or geographical features debating environmental concerns. Design costumes and create character personalities appropriate to each continent.

- **Supplemental non-writing activities** are also major assignments; many are appropriate for group tasks, for example:

  Design and construct papier-mâché models of organs. Create mini-posters describing the parts and functions of each organ and set up an organ museum.

date

Dear Parent:

I am pleased to announce that your child will be involved in a journal writing program in my class this year. The students will write in their journals at least twice each week about specified topics that often pertain to our regular studies. The topics they are assigned will be designed to improve their understanding of our subject matter and at the same time their writing skills, while also providing creative challenges.

The students will be required to turn in some, but not all, of their journal entries. For the entries they are required to turn in, there will be a Required Topic Cover Sheet which outlines the assignment and specific skill areas to be assessed. Many of the entries which are not turned in help the students prepare for required assignments; a student's failure to keep up with all of the journal entries will be reflected in the papers which are turned in. Although I will not collect every journal entry, I will check frequently to see that students are maintaining their journals.

Your child will need a three-ring binder in which to keep all journal entries and all papers associated with the journal activities. This binder must be brought to class every day. You may want to require that it be brought home each evening so your child can add to it as part of his or her daily homework routine. After all, writing improves with regular practice.

Please ask to see the journal regularly to gauge what your child is learning and how his or her writing is improving. Your interest and encouragement are the greatest motivators for your child.

To start the journal program, your child has determined some goals which are indicated on the attached sheet. Please read these goals, add your comments or suggestions, sign the form, and have your child return it to me. After I add my comments, the goals sheet will be placed in your child's journal binder.

I look forward to working with you and your child this year, and I hope that you will contact me if you have any questions or comments.

Sincerely,

My Journal Writing Goals

Date ____________________

This year I plan to improve my writing in the following ways:

____
____
____
____
____
____
____
____

Parent Comments: ____________________________
____
____
____
____

Teacher Comments: ____________________________
____
____
____
____

________________ (Student Signature) ________________ (Parent Signature) ________________ (Teacher Signature)

Required Topic Cover Sheet

Name ______________________________

Assignment # ____________ Date ______________

Title ____

Purpose:

_____ Narrative

_____ Descriptive

_____ Informative

_____ Analytical

Special Attention Areas:

Mechanics ______________________________

Organization ______________________________

Style ______________________________

Content ______________________________

Audience:

General _____ Specific______________________ Date Due____________

Assignment: Using information you have learned from our work in class, describe as fully and as clearly as you can the following topic:

____

(Insert your topic description here.)

Use this sheet for your preliminary notes and rough copy; attach any extra sheets as needed. Finally, when you are ready to submit your edited draft, attach your best copy to this sheet.

Record of Required Topics

Name______________________________

Topics	Date Due	Date Completed

Specific Skill Areas

Name ____________________________

Throughout the year you will be writing many different types of papers in your journal. I expect you to do your best work on all of these papers, including carefully proofreading each one to find and correct all errors. These are the types of mistakes that you should be able to recognize on your own:

- simple spelling mistakes
- missing or improper punctuation
- omitted or repeated words
- presence of incomplete or run-on sentences

For some journal entries we will focus special attention on particular skills. In these cases, you will record the specific skills for the entry, along with other information about the assignment on the cover sheet for the journal entry. The specific skill areas fall generally into these four basic categories:

Mechanics

Correct capitalization

Proper use of punctuation

Proper use of quotation marks

Standard usage (subject-verb agreement)

Style

Vocabulary appropriate to aim and audience

Varied sentence structures

Rhetorical and literary devices

Point of view and tone of voice

Organization

Developing effective topic sentences

Proper sequencing of details

Appropriate essay structure (introduction, body, conclusion)

Building logical paragraphs

Constructing appropriate transitions

Content

Accuracy

Logic

Use of details

Credibility

Since we will refer to these areas throughout this year, you should save this sheet in your JOURNAL and become familiar with each of these skill areas. You should use this sheet as a proofreading checklist for all of your writing assignments including those for which no specific skill areas are designated. You will also need this sheet when you are asked to select your own specific skill areas on which to focus for an assignment.

If you have any questions about any of these concepts, or about your writing, don't be afraid to ask!

Proofreading and Correction Symbols

Name ______________________________

Symbol	Meaning
○	A circle around a word indicates a spelling error.
□	A square around a word indicates a misspelling of a "Troublesome Word." The letters TW may also be written above the square.
∧	A caret of this sort indicates missing punctuation, letter(s), or word(s). The missing punctuation, letter, or word will be added.
Cap.	Capitalize this letter.
lc	Lowercase this letter.
Awk.	Short for the term "awkward," this abbreviation indicates awkward or strained phrasing. Look for an easier way to phrase your thought.
//	Vertical parallel lines indicate a need for parallel construction.
¶	A two-legged, backward "P" indicates the need for a new paragraph.
WC	These letters, which stand for "word choice," indicate that you have used the wrong word. The letters followed by a question mark (WC?) indicate that your word choice is not necessarily wrong, but that you could find a better word.
Fragment	This indicates an incomplete sentence.
Run-on	Your sentence goes on . . . and on . . . and on . . .
Tense Shift	This tells you that you have changed verb tenses.
Agr.	This abbreviation means you should check your subject-verb agreement.
Unref.	This abbreviation tells you that you have used a pronoun without a readily identifiable antecedent or reference. Your reader cannot tell for sure what the pronoun represents.
Dang.	This abbreviation indicates you have misplaced a modifier and left it dangling by itself.

Troublesome Words

Name

These are troublesome words, which students often misspell or misuse in their papers. Keep this list in the front of your JOURNAL and refer to it as you proofread your papers. You will be adding to this list as the year progresses.

Could (should/would) have

Its

It's

Know

No

Knew

New

Than

Then

There

Their

They're

Threw

Through

To

Too

Two

Your

You're

Affect

Effect

Journal Entry Log

Name____________________

Date	Today I Wrote About . . .

Student Self-Assessment: Required Topic

Name ____________________

Title ____________________ Date __________

1. I turned in the assignment on time. YES NO
2. I proofread this paper before handing it in. YES NO
3. Someone else proofread my work before I handed it in. YES NO

   (If YES, who?____________________)
4. Describe how well you think you did on each of the specific skill areas.

   Mechanical: ____________________

   Organizational: ____________________

   Stylistic: ____________________

   Content: ____________________
5. What is your overall opinion of your performance on this paper?

   ____
6. How do you think you can improve on the next paper? ____________________

(Use the back of this sheet if you need more space for your answers.)

Student Self-Assessment: Mid-Year

Date ______________ Name ______________________________

1. My goals for writing this year are: (Summarize from your Journal Goals sheet.)

____
____
____

2. I have improved . . . ______________________________

____
____

3. I need more work on . . . ___________________________

____
____
____

4. My favorite journal entry so far is . . . ______________

because ______________________________________

____

5. My best journal entry so far is . . . ________________

because ______________________________________

____

6. I would change or add to my goals for the rest of the year by . . . ________

____
____
____

(Use the back of this sheet if you need more space for your answers.)

Student Self-Assessment: End-of-the-Year

Date ________________ Name ________________________________

1. My goals for writing this year were: (Summarize from your Journal Goals sheet.)

____

____

____

2. I have improved . . . ____

____

____

3. I need more work on . . . ____

____

____

4. My favorite journal entry this year was . . . ______________________________

5. My best journal entry this year was . . . ______________________________

6. The goals I would set for my journal writing next year are . . . ______________

____

____

7. I feel this journal writing program has/has not helped me become a better writer

   because . . . ____

____

8. My suggestions for making this journal writing program better in the future are . . .

____

____

(Use the back of this sheet to continue your answers.)

Peer-Assessment Form

Date ______________ Name ______________________________

I read a paper entitled ______________________________

that was written by ______________________________

The best part of this paper was ______________________________

____

The following are three other things I liked about this paper:

1. ______________________________
2. ______________________________
3. ______________________________

The following are three ways I think this paper could be improved:

1. ______________________________
2. ______________________________
3. ______________________________

I READ A PAPER ENTITLED:

Things I Fed My Dog Last Week

THAT WAS WRITTEN BY:

Anthony Fiorino

THE BEST PART OF THIS PAPER WAS:

LIKE, YOU KNOW, THE END.

RIDER

(Use the back of this sheet if you need more space.)

My Body

Middle school students are fascinated by issues concerning the human body. They seek to understand the physical and emotional changes they and their friends are experiencing as they grow from children into young adults, and they continually adjust their self-concepts accordingly. What better place to start understanding who they are than by understanding how their own bodies work? Many middle school curricula include units on the human body, either in science or in health courses.

The Circulatory System

Simple Entries

- Define the function of the circulatory system in one sentence.
- Name the parts of the circulatory system.
- List the parts of the circulatory system in order.
- Sketch and label the pathway of blood flowing through the heart.
- For each step in the pathway of blood through the heart, list three appropriately descriptive sensory adjectives.
- List activities that are beneficial to the heart.
- List activities that are detrimental to the heart.

Short Paragraphs

- Write a paragraph describing the pathway of blood through the heart.
- Using sensory adjectives (see *Simple Entries*), write a paragraph or poem describing the journey of blood through the heart.
- Imagine that you are a blood cell and describe as fully as you can your experience of flowing through the heart.
- How would a blood cell change during one complete cycle through the body?
- If the heart were a person, what would his/her personality be like? Explain.
- If the heart were a person, describe what kinds of jobs it might seek.
- Describe the differences between a red corpuscle and a white corpuscle.
- Which would you rather be, a red blood cell or a white blood cell? Tell why.

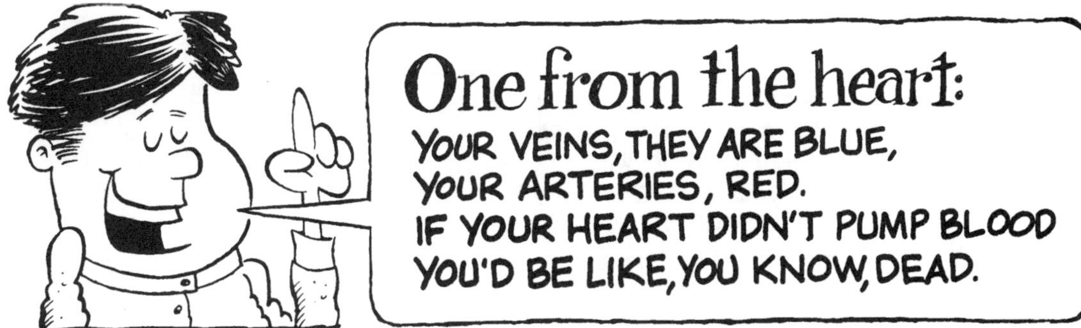

The Circulatory System (Cont.)

Longer Tasks

- Compare the circulatory system with a river system, describing the similarities and differences between the two systems.
- How is the circulatory system like a system of roads? How is it different?
- Write a conversation that blood cells might have with one another as they circulate through the body.
- If the heart could talk to the brain, what would it say? Write out their conversation.
- Pretend the heart is a museum and you are a tour guide for visiting blood cells. Take us along on your tour.
- Take us on a bus tour around the circulatory system. Be sure to point out all the important sites!
- It is Career Day in Blood Cell School, and you are the guest speaker. Tell us about your job. What does it take to be a vital, functioning blood cell?
- Using a first person monologue, describe what a heart might experience as its owner participates in a beneficial or detrimental activity.
- Imagine that your heart is a person looking for a job and write your heart's resume.
- Describe an interview between your heart and a prospective employer.
- Develop an argumentative essay to convince a reader that the heart is the most important organ in the human body.
- Describe as fully as possible how your digestive system relies on the circulatory system.

The Respiratory System

Simple Entries

- What is the function of the respiratory system?
- List the parts of the respiratory system.
- Sketch and label the parts of the respiratory system.
- List the functions of each part of the respiratory system.
- List the major components of the air we breathe. Underline those your body uses and circle those your body does not use.
- List sensory adjectives to describe what it would be like inside your lung.
- List sensory adjectives to describe what it would be like inside an alveolus.
- List possible ailments of the respiratory system.
- List manufactured objects which need to bring in air in order to operate.

Short Paragraphs

- Describe in 25 words or less the difference between internal (cellular) respiration and external (breathing) respiration.
- Which is more important, internal or external respiration? Explain.
- Explain why you can "see your breath" in cold weather.
- How is the respiratory system like a stream? How is it different?
- If you had to make a larynx, what materials would you use?
- Your larynx is most like which musical instrument(s)? Explain.
- If you were your epiglottis, how would you describe your job?
- How are lungs similar to, yet different from, gills?
- What might your lungs say to one another if they could talk?
- How does the respiratory system rely on the circulatory system?
- If your body were an internal combustion engine, what part of that engine would the respiratory system be? Explain your answer.

The Respiratory System (Cont.)

- How is your respiratory system like/unlike that of . . .

  a paramecium? an earthworm? a grasshopper? a fish? a bird?
- Explain why some people snore.

Longer Tasks

- Write a dialogue between your trachea and your esophagus. How would they compare and contrast their jobs?
- Describe what you would see, hear, and feel if you were hang-gliding your way through the respiratory system.
- Explain how cellular respiration is similar to the furnace in your home.
- Compare and contrast your respiratory and circulatory systems with respect to functions, parts, and processes.
- Prepare a travel brochure describing a vacation in the lungs.
- Write an adventure story in which a heroic oxygen molecule must brave the dangers of the respiratory system to save a carbon dioxide molecule in distress, held captive by a wicked alveolus.
- Write an episode for the soap opera series "As I Live and Breathe," using respiratory system organs as thecharacters.

The Digestive System

Simple Entries

- In twenty-five words or less, define the function of the digestive system.
- Sketch and label the parts of the digestive system in order, from the mouth to the small intestine.
- List the digestive organs, the digestive enzymes that come from each, and the function of each enzyme.
- List adjectives to describe what it would be like inside your mouth.
- List the flavor characteristics that your tongue can distinguish. Tell which part of the tongue is associated with each flavor characteristic.
- Draw a food group pyramid or list the basic food groups. Tell what your favorite/least favorite food from each group is.
- List adjectives to describe what it would be like inside the stomach, including an adjective for each of the five senses.
- If you were a villus in the small intestine, which elements of the food stream would you absorb, and which would you reject?

Short Paragraphs

- Describe a trip into a mouth as if you were a miniature spelunker (caver).
- Become a piece of food and travel through the system from the mouth to the small intestines. Describe what you see and experience along your trip.
- What does your digestive system have in common with a ____________ (another animal)? How is it different?
- How would your teeth describe your favorite food?
- What would it be like inside your small intestine? Inside a villus?
- If you were one of the villi in your small intestine, how would you describe your job?
- How are the villi of the small intestine similar to the alveoli of the lungs?

The Digestive System (Cont.)

Longer Tasks

- Imagine that all the parts of the digestive system are debating among themselves which one is the most important. Describe their debate.
- You are a reporter for "Health Beat" on your local TV station. Interview an organ of the digestive system.
- Describe the parts of the digestive system as if they were rides at an amusement park.
- If you had to design a digestive system using items you could buy in a department store, what items would you use and why? (Students could also illustrate how the items would be used in the digestive system.)
- Imagine that your tongue and your stomach are food critics. How might each critique the contents of your last meal? What might each consider the "Perfect Meal?"
- Design the instruction manual for a "Do-It-Yourself Digestive System" kit.
- Select a part of the digestive system and write a "Dear Abby" letter seeking advice for a particular problem it might have. Write the response. (This could also be done effectively with pairs of students who exchange letters and then write the responses.)

The Excretory System

Simple Entries

- List the parts of the excretory system.
- List the functions of each part of the excretory system.
- Which parts of the excretory system function in connection with other systems?
- Sketch a kidney and label the parts.
- List sensory adjectives to describe what it would be like to be a Bowman's capsule in a kidney.
- List all the elements in blood that are filtered in the kidneys. Which are returned to the blood? Which are removed?

Short Paragraphs

- Describe the functions of the excretory system in a short paragraph.
- What would happen if your kidneys stopped functioning?
- Where do most waste products come from, and how do they get to the excretory system?
- Write a "Want Ad" for a kidney.
- Write a short "Thank You" note to your kidneys.

Longer Tasks

- Write a poem entitled "Ode to a Bladder."
- Write a short story describing an ammonia molecule's harrowing escape from your body.
- Describe how the kidneys are like a wastewater treatment plant.
- Write a conversation between your kidneys and your large intestine. Tell how they would compare their jobs.

The Skeletal System

Simple Entries

- List the major sections of the skeleton and name some major bones contained in each.
- List the bones in your . . .

  arm

  wrist/hand

  leg

  skull

  ankle/foot

  chest

  spine

  ear

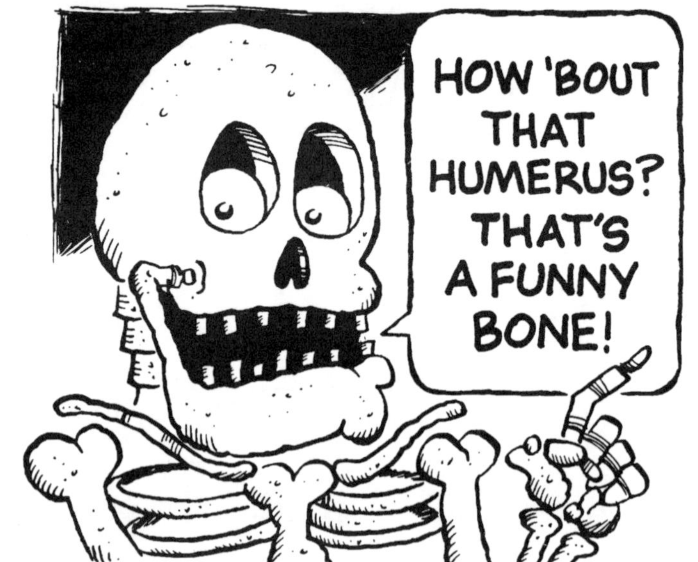

- Sketch and label the major parts of any bone structure.
- List three areas of your body that are made of cartilage, not bone.
- List the three types of joints in the body and give an example of each.
- List all the functions of the skeletal system.
- List five things you could not do if you didn't have a skeleton.
- List problems or diseases that can damage your skeleton.
- List five foods or nutrients that are particularly important for bones.

Short Paragraphs

- Explain the difference between a tendon and a ligament.
- Explain what cartilage is and why it is important.
- Select one type of joint and describe how it works by comparing it to something which is not part of a living organism.

The Skeletal System (Cont.)

- Describe how bones are related to the circulatory system.
- What is your favorite bone? Explain.
- What is the most important bone in your body? Explain.
- What is the least important bone in your body? Explain.
- Describe the difference between the axial and the appendicular skeleton.
- Write a short "Want Ad" for a particular bone.
- If the bones in your body were members of a football team, and you were the coach, which bones would you choose to play each position? Explain.
- Describe how a broken bone heals.

Longer Tasks

- Describe what life might be like if your body had no skeleton.
- Imagine you are an alien scientist. You have never seen a human being. You come across a human skeleton. How would you describe it? How could you determine probable characteristics of humans based on the skeleton?
- Describe a trip through the Haversian canals as though you were a blood cell.
- Write a dialogue between a ligament and a tendon, both of which are located near the knee. (Substitute any other major joint as desired.)
- Write a set of instructions for assembling a skeleton as though it were a model kit.
- You are the play-by-play announcer at a football game in which all the players are bones. Call the game played between the Axial team and the Appendicular team. (Other sports can readily be substituted here.)
- Describe a day in the life of a bone.
- Write a poem to a bone.
- Select a particular bone and write it a "Thank You" note for the ways it helps you.

The Skeletal System System (Cont.)

- Describe how you might use the bones and joints of a skeleton to make some other object.
- Describe how your skeleton might be different if you spent all or most of your life in . . .

  trees.

  water.

  space.
- Describe how a skeleton changes as it ages. Write this in the form of an inter-generational converstion between an infant's skeleton, a teenager's skeleton, an adult's skeleton, and an octogenarian's skeleton.

DUUDE... LIKE, WHAT KIND OF SKELETON WOULD YOU HAVE IF YOU SPENT ALL YOUR TIME ON A, LIKE, SKATEBOARD?

The Muscular System

Simple Entries

- List the functions of muscles?
- List at least five activities that are carried on by involuntary (smooth) muscles.
- List the three major types of muscles and give an example of each.
- List major muscles of . . .

  the arms.

  the legs.

  the torso.

  the head, neck, and face.

- List adjectives you might use to describe muscles.
- What supplies must your muscle cells receive in order to function properly?
- List benefits of exercise.
- List problems that might impede muscle function.

Short Paragraphs

- Explain what a tendon is and what it does?
- Explain how flexors and tensors work together.
- Explain the difference between smooth muscles and skeletal muscles.
- If you had to be a smooth muscle, which one would you be and why?
- If you had to be a skeletal muscle, which one would you least like to be and why?
- Describe what it might be like inside a muscle cell.
- Tell what a muscle cell might think about while it is working.
- Tell what a muscle cell might dream about when it is at rest.

The Muscular System (Cont.)

- What is the most important muscle in the body? Defend your choice.
- If you were going to create a working model of a skeletal muscle, tell what materials you might use and why.
- Describe what happens to muscles when you exercise.
- Describe what happens to muscles when you do not exercise.
- Describe how your muscle feels after it has been working for a long time.

Longer Tasks

- Describe in detail a day in the life of a skeletal muscle.
- Describe in detail a day in the life of a smooth muscle.
- Write a dialogue between two muscle cells in your biceps as they participate in an arm wrestling contest.
- Select a skeletal muscle, then describe what it would be like to lose the use of that muscle.
- Describe how your muscular and circulatory systems rely on each other.
- Describe the personality of a cardiac muscle.
- Imagine that a skeletal muscle goes looking for a job. What type of job would it seek? What might it say in a job interview?

The Muscular System (Cont.)

- If muscles could talk, describe a conversation they might have with each other?
- If your heart went shopping for clothes, what type of outfit would it most likely buy? Describe its shopping trip.
- Your brain and your heart are in the grocery store. Describe their conversation as they debate which foods to buy.
- Describe the major muscles involved in your favorite sport and the movements those muscles must make.
- Imagine that you have been weightless in space for a long time, and then describe your first moments back in a gravitational environment.
- You are the gossip columnist for *The Body News.* Write a column describing the activities of various muscle "celebrities."
- Try to write a detailed set of muscle instructions for a simple action. For example, think of all the muscles needed to open a jar, turn on a light, pick up a dime, or whistle a tune.

The Nervous System

Simple Entries

- List and define the three major parts of the nervous system.
- Draw and label the parts of a nerve cell.
- List the functions of the nervous system.
- List the major sections of the brain and tell what each controls.
- Draw a picture of the brain and label its major structures.
- List the five senses and the sense organ responsible for each.
- List the major parts of one of the sense organs.
- Synesthesia is the mixing of sensory images. For example, what color is violin music or what is the taste of purple? Make up a list of at least five such questions. (Student can also answer each of their own questions, or lists can be exchanged among students.)
- For each of the senses, name at least one animal in which that sense is more developed than in humans. (Example: Hawks have a keener sense of sight than humans.)

Short Paragraphs

- Explain what happens when a nerve cell receives a stimulus.
- Describe briefly how your life might change if you lost one of your senses.
- Which of the five senses do you think is the most important? Explain.
- If you had to give up one of your senses, which one would you choose and why?
- Describe a recent meal using as many sensory adjectives as you can.
- Describe that same meal again, but this time employ the synesthesia technique (see *Simple Entries*). Describe the sensory details in terms of other senses.
- Write a brief description of what it might be like to live inside your eye or your ear.

The Nervous System (Cont.)

- Compare and contrast the roles played by rods and cones in your eyes.
- Which portion of the nervous system is most important? Explain.
- Write an argument to convince your readers that the nervous system is the most important system in the human body.
- Explain how your nervous system is different from that of . . .

  an earthworm.

  a shark.

  a bird.

  a cat.

- Describe how a nerve impulse travels across a synapse.

Longer Tasks

- Write a conversation that might occur between two nerve cells.
- Compose a hypothetical debate among the five senses, each of which believes it is the most important.
- You are a nerve impulse (message). Describe in detail your journey from a receptor cell to the spinal cord or the brain and back to a muscle.
- Write a short mystery story in which each major clue requires the use of a different sense.
- Write a myth to explain why we have five senses, not four, or six, or ten. (For variation: write a myth explaining how humans got a particular sense, or explaining why a particular animal has a more developed sense than we do.)
- Try to describe a friend of yours in as much detail as possible. Be sure to use all of your senses.
- Describe yesterday from your brain's point of view.
- Using only one of your five senses, what have you done so far today?

The Endocrine System

Simple Entries

- What is the function of the endocrine system as a whole?
- List the major glands of the endocrine system and the general location and basic function of each.
- List the major hormones associated with each gland.
- List major conditions that can be caused by malfunctions of the endocrine system.
- If your body were a city, what business would each gland represent?

Short Paragraphs

- Select a gland and describe its function in a poem.
- If the endocrine system were a sports team (sport of your choice), what position on that team would each gland play?
- Select a gland and describe how your life would be different without it.
- Which gland is the most important? Defend your choice.
- What is diabetes, and how is it controlled?
- Write a conversation between any two or three glands.

Longer Tasks

- Describe the major glands as if you were the emcee and they were the contestants in a talent contest.
- Take us on a celebrity house tour of the endocrine system. Be sure to tell us all about the famous hormones who reside in each gland.
- Describe the entire endocrine system as if its parts were attractions of a major metropolis.
- Describe how your endocrine system has helped make you what you are today.

The Reproductive System

Simple Entries

- What is the basic function of the reproductive system?
- List the main parts of the male and female reproductive systems.
- List secondary changes that occur in a human body as it reaches maturity.
- List the steps along the path that a sperm travels from the testes to its exit from the body.
- List the steps along the path that an egg travels after its release from a follicle in the ovary.
- List the stages of a fertilized egg in its first two weeks.
- List the basic stages of embryonic development.
- List the basic stages of the birth process.

Short Paragraphs

- Tell how male and female reproductive systems are similar and different.
- Describe the journey of a sperm cell or an egg cell.
- What is the difference between mitosis and meiosis?
- Explain why sperm and egg cells have only half the usual number of chromosomes.
- Explain the difference between recessive and dominant genes.
- Explain how two brown-eyed parents can have a blue-eyed child.
- Explain the difference between identical and fraternal twins.

Longer Tasks

- Write a conversation between two sperm cells on their journey to fertilize an egg cell.
- Describe what an egg cell might be thinking about as it awaits fertilization.
- Describe from a fetus's perspective its nine months of development.
- Describe the birth process from the point of view of the . . .

  mother. father. baby. doctor.
- Tell how a newborn baby might describe its first view of the world.

Supplemental Activities

Writing Activities

The Fantastic Voyage: Using information you have learned from your studies of the human body, describe as fully and as clearly as you can the experiences of a person who is miniaturized and then travels through a human body to correct a specific ailment. You must include at least five systems in your journey and your path through the body, including entering and exiting, must be anatomically accurate.

- Be as descriptive as you can. Be there! Make your reader see, hear and feel what it might be like *inside* a human body.
- Design a cover for your story and include it on the front of your final draft.
- Include within your final draft at least one captioned illustration.

The Trial: You are a court stenographer and you are recording the proceedings of a trial at which a person is being tried for an unhealthy habit he or she has. All the witnesses are parts of the person's body. Give the witnesses names and personalities, and have their testimony reflect their functions in the body. Include some courtroom sketches to illustrate the trial. (This could also be written as a play to be performed.)

The Alien Anatomy Lesson: Imagine that you are an alien biologist from another planet. You have just returned from visiting Earth for the first time. How might you describe the human body and the systems within it to your students back on Zorf? (This could also be written as a play to be performed.)

The Body Salesman: Imagine that you are a salesperson who sells bodies to wandering souls. How would you pitch the advantages of a human body to a spirit looking for a new home?

Body Trek: Write an episode of *Body Trek: The Inner Frontier* using the human body systems as characters. Give the systems appropriate names and personalities. Create a health-related crisis for the crew to solve. (This could be written as a play or as a comic book with illustrations.)

Supplemental Activities (Cont.)

Non-Writing Activities

Models: Design and construct papier-mâché models of organs. These can be accompanied by mini-posters describing the parts and functions of the organs, and an organ museum can be set up.

Life-Size "Door Person": On a large sheet of paper, trace one of the students in the class. Hang the traced outline on a closet or room door. Use posterboard to make major parts of each of the human body systems and attach the cut-out parts to the outline in their proper location. Voilá, Doorperson!

Body Maps: Design life-size drawings of the human body systems stylized to look like a road map. (This can be used in conjunction with several of the writing exercises previously described.)

Body Systems Game: Design a board game using the circulatory system, the digestive system, or all the systems of the body. Incorporate health problems and remedies and include rules for playing the game. Make mini-organs for the game pieces.

Human Body Jigsaw Puzzles: Make a life-size human body jigsaw puzzle out of corrugated cardboard or thin plywood. On the back of each organ write the name of the system to which it belongs and a description of the function that organ fulfills. This project, a more challenging version of Door Person (see above), can become a permanent teaching display in your classroom particularly if it is made of plywood.

Organ Music: Working in groups, make up songs describing the functions of systems or organs of the body. Compose original music or use existing melodies. Hold a concert and videotape it.

Body Shirts: Using permanent fabric markers or fabric paint, draw an outline of a human body on both the front and back of a plain T-shirt. On the back, draw the skeletal system and the nervous system on one half of the body, and the muscles on the other half. On the front of the shirt, draw the circulatory and digestive systems. Have a "shirt day" when students wear their shirts to school. (As a variation, different students can draw different systems, one per shirt.)

Body Mobiles: Design and construct single- or multiple-system mobiles based on the organs of each system. From each suspended organ, hang a title and a brief description of what the organ does. Hang the mobiles from the ceiling.

My Place in History

Understanding who we are, involves understanding our common past. Journal writing activities can help students see history as human endeavors and accomplishments of real people just like themselves, not just facts in a book.

The Big Picture

Simple Entries

- List as many major civilizations that no longer exist as you can.
- List similarities and/or differences between ______________________________ .
  (specify any two civilizations)
- List the natural resources that were available to the people in ______________________ civilization.
- List ways in which the people of the ______________________ civilization used their natural resources.
- If the ____________________ civilization had had newspapers, list possible headlines that might have been written.
- If the ____________________ civilization had had magazines, what might some titles have been?
- Imagine that you were living in the __________________ civilization, and you decided to bury a time capsule for future people to open and learn about your culture. What items would you have included? Explain.

Short Paragraphs

- Describe in detail the clothing worn by people in the ____________________ civilization.
- Describe a day in your life if you had lived in the ______________ civilization.
- If you could travel back in time to any civilization, which civilization would you choose and why?
- If you were to travel back to ___________________________ civilization, what might be the greatest difference between life then and now?
- Compare how people in the ________________________ civilization used their resources with the ways we use ours today.
- What would you say to a person from the ____________________ civilization if through some strange technology, you could communicate with each other?
- Imagine you have just arrived via time machine in ____________________ . The chronometer on your time machine says ______________. Describe what you see as you emerge from the time machine.
  (year)

The Big Picture (Cont.)

Longer Tasks

- Record a conversation between representatives of ________________________ . (Specify any two cultures or civilizations.)
- If you could eavesdrop on a conversation between two people in the ________________________ culture, record their conversation.
- Tell how a common person in the ________________________ culture might have felt about the leader(s) or the government at that time?
- Select one of the headlines you listed (see *Simple Entries*) and write the featured article.
- Imagine that you are an art critic for one of the magazines (see *Simple Entries*). Write a critique of the art of your day. (You could use a specific artist, if one is known for the period in question.)
- Select a civilization and convince your readers that it was the greatest civilization to ever have existed.
- Describe what you think teenagers did for fun in ________________________ .
- If you were able to talk with any historical personality, who would that person be? Why? What would you talk about? (Indicate whether students can choose anyone or if they are limited to a particular culture or time being studied.)

Exploration and Colonization

Simple Entries

- List reasons why European nations wanted to colonize the Americas.
- List major inventions or advancements that made world exploration possible by the late 1400s.
- List major countries involved in colonization of the Americas, and tell what areas each colonized.
- If you were a colonist from ________________ , list reasons why you chose to come to the Americas.
- List as many ways you can think of that demonstrate how life in a colony would be different from life in Europe in the ___ century.
- List as many ways you can think of that demonstrate how Native American living differed from European living in the ____ century.
- List the colonies in order of their settlement.
- List differences between northern and southern colonies.
- Select a colony and list the advantages it might have offered settlers.
- As a colonial leader, list conditions you might have looked for as a suitable place to locate your colony.

Short Paragraphs

- Explain which invention or advancement was most influential in starting the European age of exploration?
- Imagine you are one of the following explorers: Columbus, Henry Hudson, Ponce de Leon, Balboa, or Cortez. Write a brief ship's log entry for the first day you reach the New World.
- Imagine you are a colonist on your voyage from Europe to America in the year _______ . Describe one of the following:
  - the voyage itself and life aboard ship
  - your hopes, fears, and expectations for life in America
  - your first view of the New World

Exploration and Colonization (Cont.)

- Tell how a TV reporter might have covered Columbus's "discovery" of America.
- Imagine you are a Native American in the year ______. Describe your first encounter with European settlers. (Or imagine that you are a colonist meeting Native Americans for the first time.)
- If you had had to select a new colony in which to live, tell which of the original thirteen you would have chosen and why.

Longer Tasks

- Select two famous explorers and write a conversation in which each tries to convince the other that his/her discoveries were more important.
- If you were a colonial leader about to launch an expedition, describe the people and supplies you would take with you.
- Imagine you are a colonist in the year ________. Write a letter to your family or friends back in Europe describing your life here.
- Imagine you are a slave in a southern colony. Describe your life.
- Write a conversation between an indentured servant and a slave living on the same plantation.
- You are the public relations director for the ______________________________ colony. Convince a prospective settler that your colony is the best one.
- Write a story to explain what you think happened to the settlers at Roanoke in 1585.
- How might the world be different if Columbus had been lost at sea and never returned with news of the New World?
- How would setting up a colony on the moon today be similar to, yet different from, the early European colonial ventures? In which colony would you rather be a participant, and why?

On to Independence

Simple Entries

- List reasons why the colonies wanted independence. (Consult the Declaration of Independence.)
- Draw and label a map of the thirteen original colonies.
- List events that led to the American Revolution.
- Illustrate an event that led to the American Revolution.
- List, in chronological order, major battles of the American Revolution.
- List as many British and Colonial generals as you can.
- List sensory adjectives to describe a battle of the Revolutionary War.

Short Paragraphs

- Select a portion of the Declaration of Independence and rewrite it in modern language.
- Select an event that affected the American Revolution and describe its effect.
- Select a battle of the Revolutionary War and summarize its importance.
- Describe a British army uniform, a Hessian uniform, or a Colonial uniform.
- Compare and contrast the equipment used by British and Colonial soldiers.
- Describe how a musket was loaded and fired.
- Describe how Tories felt about the Revolutionary War.
- Select a famous personality from the Revolutionary War era and describe him or her. Include a brief explanation of why this person was important.
- Select a battle and tell how topography or geography played an important role in what happened.

YO ENGLAND!
WE'RE OUTTA
HERE!!

On to Independence (Cont.)

Longer Tasks

- Tell how a TV reporter might have covered the . . .

  Boston Tea Party.

  Boston Massacre.

  signing of the Declaration of Independence.

- Tell how a Native American or a slave living on a southern plantation might have felt about the American Revolution.
- You are a Colonial newspaper editor. Write an editorial either supporting or condemning the . . .

  Boston Tea Party.

  Boston Massacre.

  signing of the Declaration of Independence.

- You are Paul Revere or William Dawes. Describe your activities on the night of April 18, 1775.
- Imagine you were a *minuteman* or a British soldier standing on the village green at Lexington. Describe the scene and your feelings just before the first shot was fired.
- Select two members of the Continental Congress and write a conversation they might have had about the Declaration of Independence.
- Write a conversation between two participants in the Boston Tea Party.
- Write a letter home from the winter encampment at Valley Forge.
- Imagine you are General Washington. Write a letter to Congress explaining your loss/victory at ______________________________ (specify battle: e.g. Bunker Hill, Trenton, Brandywine, Germantown, Yorktown).

On to Independence (Cont.)

- You are young Lafayette arriving in America in September of 1777. Describe your feelings about the revolution and your first battle at Brandywine.
- Imagine you are George Washington. Write a letter home to Martha.

Dear Martha,
I cannot tell a
lie. It's cold.
Love,
George

- Write a conversation among three or more soldiers around a campfire at Valley Forge, one of whom is from Connecticut, one from Pennsylvania, and one from North Carolina.
- You are a British officer wintering in Philadelphia in 1777. Write a letter home describing your successful autumn campaign.
- You are General Cornwallis. Describe your actions and your feelings at Yorktown.
- Write a headline and a newspaper article from the American perspective for the day the Treaty of Paris was signed.
- Write the same article from a British perspective.

New Nation, New Century

Simple Entries

- List reasons why the Articles of Confederation did not work.
- List the major points in each article of the Constitution.
- List, in chronological order, major inventions of the 19th century.
- List famous participants at the Alamo.
- List Native American tribal groups who were forced off their original lands.
- List major waves of immigration to America in the nineteenth century.
- List states that entered the union between ______________ (select range of years).
- List slave states, list free states in the year 1860.
- List ways you think people's lives changed during the nineteenth century.
- List major events that led to the Civil War.
- List sensory adjectives to describe what it might have been like to be a slave on a southern plantation in 1830 . . . 1861 . . . 1865.
- List important people in the first half of the nineteenth century.
- List terms of the surrender at Appomattox.
- What major labor organizations were born in the late nineteenth century?
- What major industries developed in the second half of the nineteenth century?

Short Paragraphs

- Select one of the important people of the first half of the nineteenth century and explain why he or she was important.
- Summarize the differences between the Articles of Confederation and the Constitution from an ordinary person's point of view.
- Select an invention from the nineteenth century and explain why it was or is important from a historical perspective.
- Select an invention of the nineteenth century and explain how it changed the lifestyle of an ordinary person of that time.

New Nation, New Century (Cont.)

- Select an immigrant group and tell when and why they came to America and where most of the group settled.
- Select a Native American group and tell when, where, and why they moved during the nineteenth century.
- What do you think was the biggest difference between life in the North and life in the South before the Civil War? Explain.
- Describe the uniform of a Union soldier. (Draw one and label its parts.)
- Describe the uniform of a Confederate soldier. (Draw one and label its parts.)
- Explain why labor unions blossomed in the late nineteenth century.
- Describe a "monopoly" and give an example of one that existed in the nineteenth century.
- Explain "yellow journalism" and how it can influence people's actions?
- You are Mrs. O'Leary's cow. What do you have to say for yourself?

Longer Tasks

- You are President Jefferson. Explain to Congress why you think it is important to buy the Louisiana Territory.

New Nation, New Century (Cont.)

- Write a conversation between President Jefferson and Lewis and Clark as Jefferson sends them off on an expedition through the new Louisiana Territory.
- Lewis and Clark kept detailed journals of their trip. Imagine you are along with them and keeping a journal, too. Describe a day of your journey.
- Imagine you are Sacagawea. Describe the Lewis and Clarke expedition.
- Write a conversation between Alexander Hamilton and Aaron Burr that might have occurred shortly before their famous duel.
- You are an elderly Native American in the year 1890. Describe your life to your great-grandchildren. (Select a tribal group appropriate to your area or your particular topic.)
- Describe how you would have felt if you had been the one to discover gold at Sutter's Mill in 1848.
- Describe a day in the life of a slave in ________________________ (select era).
- You are a soldier on the eve of battle in the Civil War. Write a letter home.
- Write a conversation between Lee and Grant at Appomattox.
- Write a first-person story describing what happened at Little Big Horn in 1876. (You may select the point of view of any participant.)
- You are a worker on the Transcontinental Railroad. Write a letter home describing your work and what it was like when the lines met at Promontory Point.
- Imagine that you are Thomas Edison. Write an excerpt from your journal describing one of your inventions and the significance you expect the invention will have.
- If you had been given the opportunity to make the very first long-distance telephone call, to whom would you have placed that call, and what would you have said?
- Imagine a dinner-table conversation between Samuel Gompers and Andrew Carnegie. Write a newspaper account of it.
- Describe a visit to the Centennial Exposition in Philadelphia in 1876 or to the Chicago Exposition of 1893.

The Twentieth Century

Simple Entries

- List major inventions of the twentieth century. Circle the one you think is the most important.
- List famous people of the twentieth century.
- Make a list of at least five questions you would ask ______________________ . (Name a famous person being studied, or allow students to choose.)
- List, in chronological order, the major wars of the twentieth century.
- Name at least ten significant events, other than wars, that have occurred in your lifetime.
- List comparative adjectives to describe how the twentieth century differs from the nineteenth century.
- Make a list of the ten decades of the twentieth century. Then, create a slogan to characterize each one.
- Name at least five countries that existed in the year 1900, that no longer exist. Name five countries that exist today that did not exist in 1900.
- List the amendments to the Constitution that have been written in this century.

The Twentieth Century (Cont.)

Short Paragraphs

- Describe what you think has been the most influential invention of this century.
- Select a famous twentieth century personality and tell why you would like to meet this person.
- Select a famous twentieth century personality and describe what life might be like if this person had not existed.
- Choose a famous person of this century who had to make a major decision. Then tell why you would or would not have done the same if the decision had been yours to make.
- Using the questions you wrote for a famous person (see *Simple Entries*), try to answer one or two of those questions as you think that person might have answered them.
- Select a twentieth century amendment to the Constitution and explain how it affects you.
- You are Wilbur or Orville Wright. Describe your first flight.

Longer Tasks

- Select an important invention of the twentieth century, describe its importance, and explain how it influences your life.
- Explain how the automobile has changed life in the twentieth century. Try to account for as many influences as you can.
- Select a major event of the twentieth century and write an eye-witness account of what occurred.

The Twentieth Century (Cont.)

- Find a famous photograph from this century and describe it as you would in a phone conversation with someone who does not have access to it. Be sure to include a description of the mood it creates or the impact it has on the viewer.
- If you were to script a documentary film about life in the twentieth century, what would your film include? Describe in detail your introduction and your conclusion for this film.
- Select a major historical event that has occurred in your lifetime and describe where you were and what you were doing when that event occurred. Also describe how it has affected your life.
- Prepare both sides of a debate over a major issue of the twentieth century. Examples could include:
    - League of Nations
    - temperance movement and prohibition
    - the social security system
    - the use of the atom bomb in 1945
    - the civil rights movement of the 1960s
    - the women's rights movement and the ERA
    - women's suffrage
    - the federal income tax
    - American isolationism in the late 1930s
    - the creation of Israel
    - the anti-war movement of the 1960s
    - any current political issues
- Draw a series of political cartoons to support both positions on any of the topics listed above.

Modern Culture and Technology

Simple Entries

- List adjectives you might use to characterize modern culture.
- List inventions of the past fifteen years that have changed our culture.
- List five living people who you think are the most influential in our modern culture.
- List adjectives to describe current trends in fashion (clothes).
- List the first ten things you think a person who lived 100 years ago would notice about our modern world if he/she suddenly appeared here.
- List as many leisure activities as you can.
- List stories in today's news that could just as easily have been in the news fifty years ago. List stories which could not possibly have been in the news before the present time.
- List the defining elements of today's culture. That is, what would you say makes our culture what it is today?
- If you had to take a photograph that would capture essential features of modern culture, list the things that would be in that photo.
- List as many good things as you can about our contemporary culture.
- List major issues facing today's culture.
- If you had to move to a desert island, list three technological devices you would take with you.
- List at least five technological devices that did not exist when your parents were children.
- List the technological devices you can find in a kitchen, bathroom, or den.
- List technological devices that you think you could easily live without.
- Make up a list of hypothetical headlines that you think reflect a contemporary society.
- List what you think could be major technological advances in the next ten years.

Modern Culture and Technology (Cont.)

Short Paragraphs

- Tell how leisure activities today differ from those of _____ years ago.
- Explain how a person from the 19th century might react if he/she were somehow transported to today.
- Describe what you think is the biggest change in American culture over the last ten years.
- Explain how you think the world was different when your parents were the age you are now.
- Explain how you think people (your children?) will describe our world of today when they look back upon it in the future.
- Select one or more of the following items and describe how your life might be different if it did not exist.
    - automobiles
    - television and radio
    - electricity
    - credit card
    - telephone
    - computer
    - indoor plumbing
    - water treatment plant
    - the Constitution of the United States
    - shopping mall

- Tell what an alien from an advanced, space-traveling culture might think of our technology.
- Write a paragraph describing your solution to a major social issue in our culture.
- What technological device most symbolizes life in America today? Explain.
- Write a "Want Ad" for a technological device you would like to see someone invent.

Modern Culture and Technology (Cont.)

- What do you think was the most important technological invention of all time? Explain.
- Describe how modern technology has affected your favorite sport.

Longer Tasks

- Write a dialogue between two teenagers, one from the 1960s and one from today.
- Write a short story describing the adventures of a time traveler from the future who returns to today.
- Make a list of the items from our culture that you would include in a time capsule. Tell why you selected each item.
- Tell how a future anthropologist might interpret the items in your time capsule.
- A thousand years from now, an archeologist comes across the ruins of your town (city, neighborhood, and so on). Which structures or objects might he or she find most interesting? Why? Which might reveal the most about our culture?
- Imagine that you are that future archeologist. Write a day's entry from your log describing structures and objects you have discovered and what you think they mean.
- If you were to live for a year in a less-modern culture, what things would you miss the most? Why? What things would you not miss? Why?
- Describe a computer to someone who has never seen one—for example, Sir Isaac Newton.
- Select a major issue facing today's society. List the pros and cons of this issue. Then write a debate between two individuals, each representing one side of the issue.
- Write a short story that describes a character dealing with this major issue.
- Imagine that you are a movie producer interviewing candidates for the job of scriptwriter for a movie about modern life in America. What questions would you ask of each candidate? What would you want the writer to include in the script?

Modern Culture and Technology (Cont.)

- Select one of the headlines (see *Simple Entries*) and write the news article that would accompany that headline.
- What is your favorite contemporary song? Tell how it reflects modern life.
- What is your favorite television show? What does it tell us about contemporary life? Tell how accurate you think it is.
- Describe television to a person living in 1700.
- What would Leonardo daVinci, Ben Franklin, or Thomas Edison say if they were to visit America today?
- Explain how you think the invention of the camera may have changed the role of art.
- Sometimes technology can have effects or be put to uses not originally intended. Can you think of examples where this has been the case? Select one of these cases, and describe how the inventor(s) might feel about the way(s) their invention is being used.

My Town

Simple Entries

- List the most important buildings, streets, or landmarks in your community. Then select one of these and sketch it.
- Draw a map of your town (city, neighborhood, and so on).
- List adjectives you might use to describe your community to someone who has never been here.
- List the major geographical or topographical features of your area.
- List famous family names from your community's history.
- List immigrant groups that have settled in your area.
- List major community issues based on articles in recent local newspapers.
- List major industries or businesses in your town and region.

Short Paragraphs

- If your community were a single individual, how would you describe his/her personality? Also, describe his/her physical appearance.
- Describe what this area was probably like before your community was built.
- What topographical or geographical feature most influenced the growth of your area? Explain.
- Who were the first people to come here, and why did they decide to settle here?
- Describe the architecture of a typical home in your community.
- Describe one of the most important buildings in your community.
- What industry or business is most vital to your community? Why?
- Describe how your town or region is governed.

My Town (Cont.)

Longer Tasks

- Imagine you are living in this community in the year 2020. Explain how the community might be different.
- Imagine you are living in this community in the year _________ (date from the past). Tell how the community might have been different.
- Select a major community issue and describe how you would deal with that issue.
- If you could rebuild your community, describe the changes you would make.
- If you were the public relations officer for your community, tell how you would convince people that this is a great place to live and work.
- Design a poster campaign or a series of magazine ads to promote your town or region.
- If you were in charge of your local government, what new laws would you try to enact? Present your reasons.

Supplemental Activities

Writing Activities

Newspaper of the times: Learn all you can about an important event and about the general state of the world at the time of this event. Present your research to the class in the form of a newspaper that has four major sections—National News, World News, Editorials, and Special Features—that also include the special items listed below. Create an appropriate layout, including a banner (title), for the newspaper. Remember that your articles should reflect life as it was at the time of the topic event.

National News—At least three articles covering the events and conditions leading up to the topic event, the event itself, and the subsequent effects of the event. Create at least one map and one illustration to accompany the articles. (For added impact, include additional articles about other national events occurring around the same time as the topic.)

World News—At least two articles about events occurring elsewhere in the world around the same time as the topic event. Draw at least one illustration and one map to accompany the articles.

Editorials—At least two editorials expressing opposing viewpoints concerning the topic event.

Special Features—At least one article from each of at least three of the following feature sections:

- Arts and Entertainment
- Science and Technology
- Fashion
- Farming and Business
- Want Ads and Personals
- Sports and Comics (depending on the time period)

Supplemental Activities (Cont.)

Diaries: Create a persona living in the time period and location you are studying. Throughout your study, build a life record for your character, including information about his or her lifestyle, living conditions at the time, and major events. Write a diary from this character's point of view covering a specified portion of the character's life. (The teacher will adapt the length of time to be covered in the diary based on the depth of the study and the abilities of the students.)

Plays: Write plays about people living in the times and places you are studying. Develop scenery, props and costumes to the extent that your time and resources permit. (This could be employed as a project in its own right, or in conjunction with the diary activity listed above. An evening performance for parents or an in-school performance for other classes can be the culmination for the project. Consider videotaping the play.)

Dear Diary,
Today I, Cindy Wilson,
Queen of the Vikings,
set sail for Greenland,
which, by the way,
isn't very green.

Supplemental Activities (Cont.)

Non-Writing Activities

Vignettes: Create living history scenes, such as photographs, depicting a particular time and place. Costumes, props and scenery should be as realistic as possible, and the scene selected should make an important statement about the era.

Pictorial or Three-Dimensional Timelines: Research a person, an object (such as a building or a ship) or an event and create either drawings or a three-dimensional way of depicting it, such as a model or a sculpture. A title identifying the topic and a brief summary of its significance should appear somewhere on the time line entry. Present orally and then display in chronological sequence. (Stretch clotheslines along the classroom ceiling and hang the entries. This "hanging time line" makes an impressive display without using up classroom space. It also keeps the time line visible at all times so it can be referred to throughout your studies.)

Time Capsules: Create a time capsule of artifacts representing a particular time and place. Determine the size of the capsule and the objects in advance. Gather or make the desired objects, and write brief descriptions of what the objects reveal about the time period involved. (You can do this with any time period and any culture; you are not limited to our own culture and the future. If there are several classes, capsules without the description could be exchanged and the receiving classes could be challenged to figure out what the objects signify. Interpretations and intentions can be compared for some amusing learning!)

Supplemental Activities (Cont.)

Create-a-Colony: Create a colony based on research of a particular time and place. Select a location for your colony, decide how many people to take along and what occupations these colonists should represent. Determine the supplies your colony will require to get started, and establish rules and expectations for the colony. Present a report to the class that will represent the company or the government that chartered the colonial expedition. This "living history" report should justify all the aforementioned decisions and also relate the events, successes, and failures of the colony's first year. Present it in the first person, assuming the personalities of several of the colonists. Obviously this can be used with American history, but it could just as readily be applied to other colonizations around the world.

Living History Debates: Debates appeal to students because a debate allows students to be creative and dramatic while demonstrating their knowledge of an academic area. Debates can take many forms. For example, students can appear in costume as "representatives" of various civilizations and debate the relative significance or successes of their cultures. Students can also play the roles of characters representing the various facets of the issues involved in historical events; for example, they can debate the Declaration of Independence in the Virginia legislature, or the issue of slavery as viewed by settlers living in Kansas in the 1850s.

Living History Day: Research life in a particular civilization or period of history. Develop characters to represent the time, and plan costumes, food, and events depicting the era. Set aside a day, or part of a day, in which you will "live" your characters and their times.

My World

Middle school students generally enjoy exploring the natural world and trying to understand their role in it. After all, where we are helps determine who we are, and we define ourselves in reference to the rest of the world in which we live.

The Planet

Simple Entries

- List as many facts about the earth's size and shape as you can.
- Outline the major geologic periods of the earth's history and list a distinguishing feature for each period.
- Sketch a cut-away view of the earth and label the major layers of its structure.
- List the continents of the earth.
- Diagram and identify the layers of the earth's atmosphere.
- List the oceans and major seas of the world.
- List major mountain chains of the world.
- List major rivers of the world.
- List major deserts of the world.
- List sensory adjectives to describe what it would be like (choose one) . . .

  in a rainforest.

  in a desert.

  on a glacier.

  at the North or South Pole.

  on the tundra.

  in a volcano.
- If you were a travel agent, list the places in ____________________ (name a continent) that you might advise a client to visit.
- Name the three major categories of rocks and give an example of each.
- Name as many types of rocks as you can that are found in your area.

The Planet (Cont.)

Short Paragraphs

- Describe, in your own words, the difference between a rock and a mineral.
- Summarize the rock cycle in one complete paragraph.
- Explain what fault lines are, and why earthquakes and volcanoes frequently occur along them.
- If you had to represent one of the periods of earth's geologic history, which would you chose? Why?
- Explain, in a short paragraph, the difference between longitude and latitude.
- Explain what longitude and latitude have in common.
- Tell which layer of the earth's atmosphere you think is the most important and why.
- Select an atmospheric layer and describe it in detail. Include where it is, how thick it is, what it consists of, and what function it serves.
- Select a continent and describe it as if it were . . .

  an animal.

  a fruit or a vegetable.

  a man-made object.

  Do not use the name of the continent in your description. (These can then be read aloud and the class can guess which continent is being described.)
- If you had to become one of the continents, which might you choose to be and why?
- Describe what you think a clear sunrise would be like (choose one) . . .

  in a rainforest.

  in a desert.

  on a glacier.

  at the North or South Pole.

  on the tundra.

  at sea.

The Planet (Cont.)

Longer Tasks

- Record a conversation between ______________________ (select any two continents). How would they discuss . . .

  the weather?

  their geographical or topographical features?

  their people?

  their plants and animals?

  their natural resources?

- If the continents were people, describe what their personalities might be like.
- What might a river say to the ocean when they meet? What would the ocean reply? Write the dialogue.
- Imagine you are a tree. What kind of tree might you be, and what might a day in your life be like if you grew . . .

  at the tree line of an alp?

  on an island in the _______________ (select any ocean)?

  in a rainforest?

  in a temperate zone forest?

  in the African savanna?

  in the Everglades?

- If you were a bird flying over ______________ (select a location), describe what you might see.
- How might an alien approaching the earth for the first time describe the planet to his/her leaders back on his/her home planet?
- Which continent do you think this alien would most likely choose to land on, and how might the alien describe his/her first impression on landing there?
- If the earth and the moon were talking, what might each complain about?
- If you were the earth correspondent for the *Daily Planet* (a newspaper for the stars), what would you report about conditions on earth?

The Planet (Cont.)

- Imagine that you are a volcano. Describe how you feel just before, during, and after an eruption.
- You are in a space shuttle returning to earth. Describe in detail your trip through the layers of the earth's atmosphere.
- Describe the life cycle of a mountain condensed into a single year.
- Select at least three geologic time periods to be "guests" on your late-night talk show. What questions will you ask each of your guests? How will they respond to your questions and to each other?
- Describe what it would be like if you lived within the earth's crust, rather than on it.
- Travel back in time to any of the previous geologic time periods and describe what you see around you as you exit your time machine.
- Describe how your life would be different if you lived in the Arctic or Antarctic.

Climate and Weather

Simple Entries

- List as many forms of precipitation as you can.
- List the steps in the water cycle.
- List the adjectives for the sensations you might feel if you were . . .

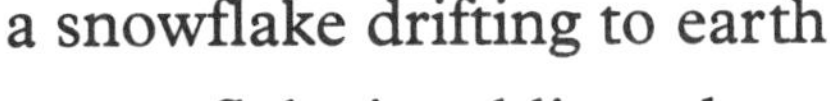

a snowflake drifting to earth.
a snowflake in a blizzard.
a hailstone forming.
a raindrop.
a bolt of lightning.
a thundercloud.
in a tornado.
in a hurricane.

- List adjectives to describe the climate and the weather of your area. (Be sure to account for any seasonal changes.)
- List major weather-related events you can remember in your lifetime.
- List ways the weather can affect everyday events and activities.
- List the major climate zones and at least one activity which is characteristic of each zone.

Short Paragraphs

- Use sensory adjectives (see *Simple Entries*) in a short paragraph to describe what it would be like to be . . .

a snowflake drifting to earth.
a snowflake in a blizzard.
a hailstone forming.
a raindrop.
a bolt of lightning.
a thundercloud.
in a tornado.
in a hurricane.

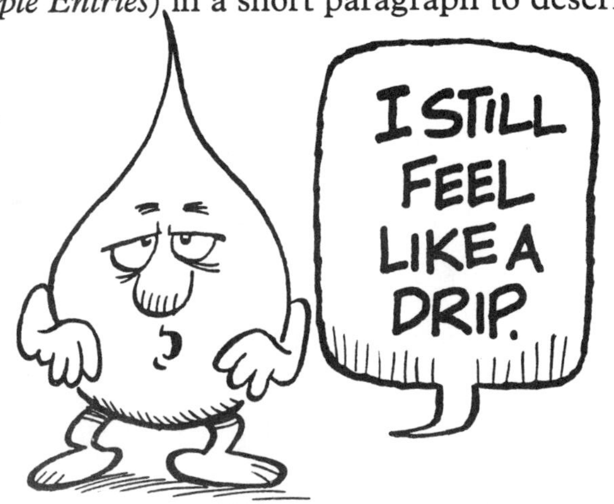

Climate and Weather (Cont.)

- Imagine a conversation between a snowflake and a raindrop. How would they compare and contrast their experiences?
- If you were a drop of water in cloud school, what might you be learning about?
- If you were a raindrop, what would you discuss with your raindrop friends . . .

  as you waited in a cloud?

  just before you fell to earth?
- What might a cold front say to a warm front as they run into each other?
- If you could be any type of cloud, what type might you be and why?
- Describe the last storm you experienced in your area.
- How is today's weather typical (or atypical) for your area?
- Which season has the best weather in your area? Defend your choice.
- Describe an experience you have had which was affected by the weather.
- In your opinion, what is the worst weather situation or condition you experience in your area? Explain why it is so bad.
- How does temperature influence life in your area? What about precipitation?
- Describe how your area might be different if the average temperature either dropped or rose by ten degrees.
- Explain how your lifestyle would change if it rained in your area most of the time.

Climate and Weather (Cont.)

Longer Tasks

- Write a story describing a water droplet's experiences in the hydrologic cycle.
- Write a newspaper article describing the effects of the worst storm you can recall.
- Describe the last time your school was closed due to the weather.
- Write a poem about today's weather.
- Write the TV weatherperson's script for today's news broadcast.
- Write a story describing what your life would be like if a major drought were to occur in your area.
- Write a myth to explain a weather phenomenon.

Ecology

Simple Entries

- List the major streams or rivers in your area.
- Define a biome. Define a niche.
- List the major biomes and tell where each is found.
- Draw and annotate a chart of the water cycle.
- Make a list of all the plants and animals that live in a particular stream or river.
- List industries in your area that use the rivers or streams.
- List adjectives to describe a local stream or river.
- Imagine you are floating down a stream on a hot summer's morning and list all the things you might see, hear, smell, and feel.
- Make a list of unusual similes involving streams. Use this form: A stream is like a ______________.
- Make a list of analogies involving streams.
- Draw and annotate a chart of the carbon-oxygen cycle (photosynthesis and respiration).
- Construct a simple food chain or food web.
- List the characteristics of a healthy stream.
- List types of pollution that can damage ecosystems. Underline those which most affect your area.
- List simple, everyday things a person can do to help the environment. Circle any you do regularly.
- Sketch at least three plants common to your area and tell where you found them.
- Name the most common trees in your area.
- Select one of the trees in your area and list the organisms that depend upon that tree in any way.

Ecology (Cont.)

Short Paragraphs

- Using the list of analogies about streams (see *Simple Entries*), write a short paragraph explaining or proving one analogy.
- Define the term *watershed* in your own words and identify the major watershed in which you live.
- Imagine a local stream or river were a person. Describe its personality.
- Tell how the water cycle affects a stream.
- Compose a haiku to capture the mood of a stream, a desert, a forest, or a glacier.
- If you were a small fish searching for a new home, what qualties would you look for in a stream? Explain.
- Describe what it would be like to be a hatching mayfly or an emerging butterfly.
- Select a niche on a food chain and explain it using first-person narrative. (You must imagine yourself as the organism occupying that niche. What do you eat? What eats you?)
- How would you solve a current pollution problem? (Choose one of the problems from *Simple Entries*, or select another problem.)
- Tell how a redwood tree would define time. Tell how an insect would define time.
- What are wetlands and why they are important ecologically?
- Describe an activity which anyone can do to help the environment.
- You are a tree. Describe in a first-person narrative what you do for a living.

Ecology (Cont.)

Longer Tasks

- Describe a complete day in the life of an aquatic organism of your choice.
- You are a river. Tell us about your journey from its headwaters to its mouth.
- Write a conversation between two second-order streams in your region that have just joined to become a third-order stream. Have them compare their respective experiences.
- Write a short skit involving the organisms living on a single rock at the bottom of a third-order stream.
- Write a conversation between an environmentalist and a person whose activities could be causing stream pollution.
- Write a letter to a government official expressing your views on the importance of streams in your community.
- You are a mountain. Describe your life cycle.
- Select a major ecological issue, such as wetlands preservation, the ozone layer, or destruction of the rainforests and write an editorial expressing your views on the issue. Be sure to provide facts to back up your argument.
- Imagine that you have been asked to write a docudrama about a particular ecosystem. Which system or biome would you select? Outline the script you would write including some ideas for camera shots and scenes you would want in your film.
- If you were the superhero, "EcoPerson," what ecological problem might you confront first? Write a story describing your struggle to overcome this problem. Include a captioned illustration with your story.
- Write about what you think the earth might be like one hundred years from now, in light of current trends in the environment.
- Describe the earth one hundred years from now in a "worst-case" scenario, that is, if environmental laws were completely overturned and abandoned.
- Describe the earth one hundred years from now as you would most like to envision it.

Supplemental Activities

Writing Activities

Planet Play: Write and perform a play in which the characters are continents or geographical features debating environmental concerns. Design costumes and create character personalities appropriate to each continent or feature.

Drop Essay: Describe as fully and as clearly as you can what it would be like to be a drop of water journeying down a local stream from its headwaters to its mouth. Give your drop a personality and make your sensory descriptions rich and full. The following items should be included in your story:

- ten geographic place names
- ten plants and/or animals
- five human uses of the stream
- three references to different chemical qualities of the stream
- five references to different physical qualities of the stream
- an annotated map of the stream showing where all of the above occur
- an illustrated cover depicting a scene from the drop's adventures

Supplemental Activities (Cont.)

Non-Writing Activities

Planetary Panorama: Design and create a panoramic mural of the continents. You can follow a standard map projection, stylize the continents as living figures, or come up with a different approach. You can paint the drawing on large rolled paper such as newsprint, on old sheets donated by parents, on ceiling tiles or directly on the walls of your room. If you opt for either of the latter suggestions, permission, plus a rough draft on paper, is highly recommended!

Pictorial Time Line: Design and create a pictorial time line of geologic history. Include a symbolic scale to show the relative duration of different eras. For each era, illustrate and caption noteworthy events such as the separation of the continents, the beginning of flowering plants, and the rise and fall of the dinosaurs.

Rock Concerts: Study a particular rock formation existing in your region. Learn all you can about the rock, its location, age, characteristics, and uses. If possible, visit a local site where you can collect samples to bring into the classroom. Then prepare a "rock concert." This "concert" must include a T-shirt showing locations where your rock can be found, an oral report presenting all the information you found in your research, and a performance of an original "rock" song that also relates important information about your rock. Your lyrics must be original, but you may use familiar melodies.

(This technique can be used with any of the topics studied. Writing and performing songs is a challenging and interesting way for students to learn, share their knowledge, and have fun. Videotape presentations if possible.)